Gerette!

The Adventures of a
Mississippi Dog in Europe

M . N . SMITH

Fulton Books, Inc.
Meadville, PA

Published by Fulton Books 2021

ISBN 978-1-63710-598-6 (paperback)
ISBN 978-1-63710-599-3 (digital)

Printed in the United States of America

My story would not be possible without the expert care of Starkville Veterinary Hospital's great team: Dr. Anthony, Dr. Shy, and their assistants. A special danke or thanks goes to Dr. Extra at Drakenmolen in Hoensbroek, Netherlands, for Stinker's diagnosis and treatment of ameloblastoma.

About the Title

Gerette (*ge-ret-tet*) means "rescued" in German! While we rescued Stinker from a terrible truck accident and abandonment, she has rescued us right back every day with her love!

—Monika Smith

Stinker's adventures began in Bradley, Mississippi, and extended to Europe.

Bradley, Mississippi
Starkville, Mississippi
Gulfport, Mississippi
Foley, Alabama
Dauphin Island, Alabama
Louisville, Kentucky
Detroit, Michigan
Germany (all over)
Belgium
Netherlands
France
Switzerland
Liechtenstein
Luxembourg
Austria
England

Saving one dog will not change the world, but surely for that one dog, the world will change forever.

—Karen Davison

My story begins on a gravel road in Bradley, Mississippi. My first humans were nice to me for a long time, well, until the truck incident. The human told his daughter that they could not afford to take me to the vet, and I probably went into the woods to die. I heard this after the ringing in my ears turned to a dull bang. They may be right, but I just had to go to a quiet place. I could not see anything. Clearly, my head ached. Actually, every bone in my body hurt!

See, I ran away from some mean dogs fighting and did not realize how close I was to the road. I did not see the truck speeding down the road. I guess the truck driver didn't see me either and couldn't stop his rear tire from running over me. I know this sounds bad, but hang on!

You see, the best thing ever is fixin' to come! I am not even sure how many days I was there because I couldn't stay awake. I do know that every time I woke up, my friend Ty was there beside me. Ty wasn't from my gravel road. He belonged to a human named Mr. Linley. They lived about a mile away, but Ty likes to come to visit all the dogs on my road and me. Ty begged me to go with him to the humans on his street. He told me that humans were on the road that took care of him and gave him treats.

When I could stand up and walk a little bit, we started our walk to his road. I could only see out of one eye, and my head was still killing me. Nevertheless, we walked. Sure enough, we were both creeping up a driveway when suddenly a human came running out of her house.

Ty said, "C'mon! There she is! She has treats!" Ty took off running toward her and got loved on. I kept walking, but I was so scared. I hurt all over, I was so hungry, and the thought of someone picking me up made me shiver.

To make a long story short, I finally let the human pick me up with a blanket. The human in a reddish brick house fed me and gave me cold water. The next thing I knew, she had me in her car seat, wrapped in a blanket, and we were driving to town.

The town was this city called Starkville. There we went to the veterinarian's clinic.

Another human gave me a treat and tried to see what the truck had done to me. It hurt so much, and the human woman who brought me there was crying. In a few minutes, the doctor human stuck me with something. Suddenly I couldn't stay awake anymore, my eyes were so heavy, and the pain was gone.

Dr. Shy, the human doctor, could not keep my eye but, he put the rest of me back together. I woke up and was in my human's arms! She was kissing my ears and petting me. I think I will rescue her; she really seems to need me. I think I will adopt her to be my mom. I will adopt the male human too and have a pop!

I like my new house with air conditioning and heat; I even have my own chair by the window and the table! I can sleep in a little bed, or I can get in bed with my humans! I have a floppy door that takes me outside whenever I want to go!

So now I am Stinker Smith, and I am thrilled Ty brought me to his neighborhood.

A picture of Stinker after surgery.

Once upon a time…

Before I go on, let me tell you a little bit about Bradley, Mississippi. Bradley is an unincorporated community in Oktibbeha County. We are like ten miles from the Walmart Supercenter in Starkville, Mississippi, and about four miles from Sturgis, Mississippi.

Starkville, Mississippi, is best known for the real *dawgs* that live at Mississippi State University. My doctor, Dr. Shy, lives there too.

Sturgis is not the famous Sturgis as in South Dakota; however, they both have motorcycle rallies each August.

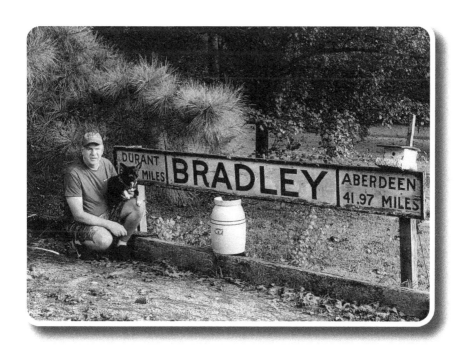

Stinker Has to Fly

Now I thought it was a long ride to see my human granny in Kentucky, but it was nothin' compared to flying to Germany—nine hours in a tin can, flyin' like a goose up in the sky! To this day, I just shake my head at the thought!

After leaving the airport in Atlanta, we flew straight to Dusseldorf, Germany. This city is neat and old. It is on the Rhine-Ruhr river. When I tell you it is old, I mean its first modern recorded population of 3,500 was in 1555. Even older than 1555, you find records showing that during the Roman Empire, Germanic tribes lived in this area!

After going through customs, Mom and I were so happy to see Pops! He met us there and drove us to our new home in a town called Gillrath. Gillrath is a farming community near Geilenkirchen, Germany. This is also home to a NATO base, which is where my pops works! "Hallo! *Wie geht es ihnen heute?*" That is German for "Hello! How are you doing today?" Here, the people stare a lot! I am not being mean. They really do! Be ready to have severe and some-times intense daily eye contact in Germany.

There is so much I want to tell you, but I do not want to bore you. So I will share ten things to know about Germany and a few of my favorite pictures. After all, a picture is worth a thousand words.

Sundays, most places are closed except between 2:00 to 4:00 p.m. This is the best time ever! Why? Because the ice cream and bak-eries are open for delicious treats. Some bigger cities may have more stores open; however, the villages keep to the Sunday tradition. This is really the second thing because the first thing was the "German stare."

The third important thing about Germany is that when they ask you how you are, they mean it—like your neighbor will take ten minutes to tell you in detail how their life has been. Be prepared!

Fourth, *do not go to a sauna*! I mean it! If you go, know that you must be *naked*! I mean n-a-k-e-d like when you were born!

Fifth, their bread will make your heart sing! They have *all* kinds of bread. It is so delicious and just thinking about it right now makes my mouth water. My aunt Mary came up to see us from Kentucky, and she loved their pretzel bread.

Sixth, those plastic cards you use in America do not work well here. They want real money, their money, not dollars. Oh, and while I am telling you about money, you will need some to go into most restrooms, get a shopping bag, or ride a shopping cart.

Seventh, if you are going to live there, you must ride a bicycle! These humans are sneaky too. The first few days when we were riding with me in a basket, of course, these really old humans passed us on a hill! It was so embarrassing for me. Later we learned that they have batteries on their bicycles, which help them peddle uphill! We usually rode our bikes to Gangelt, Germany, to eat ice cream by an old Catholic church. Later, I will tell you a neat story about Gangelt, a soldier, a village wall, and a goose. So don't let me forget.

Eighth, be prepared to see many castles in Germany as well as all over Europe. These castles can look like the ones in fairy-tale books, but some will look more like garrisons. My favorite castle was Hoensbroek Castle. We visited there many times. My new veterinarian's clinic was right across the street from the castle. Dr. Extra's clinic is called Drakenmolen, which means "dragon mill" in Dutch. You can walk through and see it set up like it could have been a long time ago. You can eat a "toasty" in the courtyard and enjoy hot tea or coffee there too!

Ninth, October festivals begin in September. Crazy, right? There is a lot of beer, but it first started as a love story. Back in 1810, the prince of Ludwig married the princess of Saxony. All the people from around the countryside were invited to come! So folks brought the extras from their fields, bread, and beer to share with all in attendance. In a way, it is kinda like our Thanksgiving in that everyone shares food.

Lastly, they let pets in the stores and restaurants! Now I must tell you that most of their dogs go to a strict obedient school early in life. I also must tell you that there are still some places we have to stay outside but not many. When my folks go to restaurants to eat, they bring me a bowl with water and a treat! Amazing! McDonald's could learn a little something from them. I am just sayin'!

Thorn, Netherlands

The Dutch flag is red, white, and blue. I have to tell you about one of my favorite places in the Netherlands, Thorn. They have the best crepes in the world! Unlike the other Dutch brick homes, this whole town is white! The bricks are painted! The reason is a clever story from long ago. St. Michaelskerk or Thorn Abby Church was started in the tenth century and ruled by girls, well by twelve church women. At one point, these women made their own coins! The town prospered! Well then, this guy name Napoleon of the French Empire conquered Thorn and that whole area. The people were made to pay taxes to the French. They even taxed the town's people by how many windows their houses had and the size of the windows. The whole town agreed to paint their houses white and camouflage the newly bricked-in windows. Clever, no? Sadly, this 1800s takeover meant all religious establishments were closed, so too was the precious little abbey.

I am almost human, see?

My auntie Mary Frances.

My European Christmas Vacation!

So our friends Sarah and Gerri spent Christmas with us in Switzerland, Austria, and Liechtenstein! We drove from Germany and through parts of France to get to Switzerland. It took us nine hours to drive to Switzerland. All vehicles must pay for a window sticker to go into Switzerland, and there are many toll roads. Austria and Liechtenstein are allies and share a border. Liechtenstein is landlocked between Austria and Switzerland. A few hundred years ago—a funny but true story—the Austrian soldiers were out on patrol when they accidentally crossed into Liechtenstein. Instead of fighting, Liechtenstein soldiers noted no one had rifles, so they just walked the Austrian soldiers back to Austria.

You know, sometimes I wonder about my friend Ty back in Mississippi and my first family. I wonder if they miss me or if they could ever believe the things I have seen. I do hope Ty is safe and warm. To know more about Austria, you must watch our favorite movie, *The Sound of Music*!

Switzerland.

The royal palace of Liechtenstein.

Tongeren, Belgium

First, I gotta tell you about french fries. Did you think they came from France? Well, you will never believe this, but it is not true. the Belgians were the first to come up with fries. Yup! They rock with waffles too! Anyway, back to my story.

This town was famous back in the Roman days; it is old too. They say that the village or town of Tongeren is Belgium's oldest town. As a Roman city, its people were the Tungri. As a matter of fact, an ancient Roman wall is still around part of the city today! It is really cool to see. They have a huge market there once a week, and my parents love to go and shop there. I love the waffle maker there. Leo gives me free waffle bites! There are still many sites to see there, especially considering that Louis XIV's troops in 1677 burned almost everything down. They began rebuilding after 1830.

Bruges and De Haan, Belgium

Chocolate! Chocolate! Chocolate! They have a giant chocolate factory there! Amazing! I counted twenty-one chocolate stores in the area. Oh, the smell! Oh, the taste! Okay, on with the rest of my story.

Bruges's story goes back to the seventh century named after a Roman bridge over the Reie River. The locals call it Belgium's Venice because of the many canals. It is gorgeous, and I will share some of my favorite pictures with you in a bit. This cute medieval town was taken by the French and later occupied by the Germans in World Wars I and II! A beautiful part of the city is the old market hall. A beautiful old church holds a gold casket with some of Jesus's blood that someone brought back from the Holy Land.

De Haan was our next stop from our three-day stay in Bruges. This was our beach trip for the Fourth of July! (By the way, no one there celebrates our Fourth of July, so no fireworks or American flags.) This beach was unlike anyone would see in Florida. I mean, the beaches had sand and water, but they also had wooden bathhouses lined up on the beach. These little, tiny changing cabins looked like old-fashioned outhouses, only fancier. A famous man named Einstein is pictured by some bathhouses. I guess he liked to visit the North Sea too. My uncle Patrick and aunt Melissa came to see us from Louisville, Kentucky. We took them to this cute boardwalk beach and ate ice cream. One more thing before we go to the next place, *De Haan* means "of the hen or chicken." This will make more sense when you see me in the pictures. My uncle Patrick and aunt Melissa loved this place too!

London, England

Off to see the queen and have fancy teatime at Harrods Department Store! Truth be told, we did not see the queen, but we saw Buckingham Palace and those cute guards. Remember the song we sing in kindergarten about the London Bridge falling down? Well, the real London Bridge is just a plain old bridge. The pretty bridge is called Tower Bridge. Now depending on where you are walking in London, you would think that there are no cafés like Belgium, France, Germany, and the Netherlands. We found cafés in small clusters, so bring snacks!

During our visit in London, a vast African cloud of dust made its way over us. The dust was so thick that it appeared to turn our two o'clock teatime into an eight o'clock night sky. Being from Mississippi, we thought the yellowish-looking sky may be tornado weather, so we parked and, of course, ate some fish-and-chips!

Have you ever heard of World War II? It was a war to save the people being killed by the Nazis. It is a complicated story to get into; however, we visited London's Underground Bunker. The bunker was used by England's leader, Churchill, to conduct the war operations during WWII. Being underground is very chilly, which was excellent in the summer but cold in the winter.

Their policemen are called "bobbies" as a nickname after Sir Robert Peel, who was like their first police chief ever! The city's coat of arms since the fourteenth century had a St. George's cross and dragon wing. Then in the seventeenth century, they added the dragon. Warning: Do *not* call *the* dragon a griffin or a gryphon because the English will take you to school!

World War II Memorials

If you do not know about this big war, you need to ask your humans because it was an incredibly important war. The first place I am going to tell you about is an American cemetery we found in the country of Luxemburg. Years after the war, a great general named Patton visited there and was killed in a car accident. Now he is buried with all the other fallen soldiers, and the place is kept beautiful in their honor.

The French and the Belgians keep many records of the Americans who fought and died in their countries. They will spend all day with you, trying to find your lost loved one. The Belgians celebrate September 11 because on September 11, 1945, they were liberated from the Nazi Germans.

The third cemetery we visited was Henri Chapelle in Belgium. There in the little Belgium office, we looked up Pops's great uncle who died in WWII. The people were so helpful, and again, the whole grounds were kept so beautifully. My humans went back on Memorial Day to place over a thousand American and Belgium flags on adopted graves. We went there as guests of Marcel and Matilda Schmetz. This sweet family turned their old farmhouse into a museum! It is called the Remember Museum. Theirs is a sweet and familiar story for those times. Mr. Marcel was about eight years old when his family assisted and cared for American soldiers. My aunt Mary loved the museum and the cemeteries.

The Netherlands has an American cemetery too. Because my mom has unique papers on me, I could go in, and she held me most of the time. Everyone has to be really quiet. This cemetery is found in the small town of Margraten, Netherlands. My uncle Patrick and aunt Melissa visited there with us.

In Berlin, Germany, we visited the Holocaust Memorial to the Jews of Europe. It was a cloudy, gray, rainy day, a day much like our hearts seeing this sad part of world history.

Mon Paris, France!

This picture was taken by Pops in front of the Arc de Triomphe, just across from this huge, underground museum, the Louvre.

Paris, France, was pretty, but many of the streets and sidewalks were filthy. This picture has the Arc de Triomphe du Carrousel. It was built to commemorate the victory of Napoleon after the Austerlitz Battle of 1805.

We took a train from Germany to Paris; it was a fun trip! The train went so fast you just saw streaks of houses! My mama thought they should slow down, but they didn't!

The Louvre is covered by a huge glass dome. At sunset, the sun's reflection makes the Louvre's dome look golden yellow. Thomas Jefferson said, "A walk about Paris will provide lessons in history, beauty, and in the point of life." My favorite artwork there was from the artist Monet. It is called *Water Lilies*. It was like he saw and painted the lilies in our pond back in Bradley, Mississippi!

They have this massive tower in Paris, and it is surrounded by a park. The Eiffel Tower has lasted for many years, surprisingly good for a temporary decoration for the 1889 World Fair! If you go there, beware of pickpockets! It was in front of the Notre Dame Cathedral where we were robbed!

The Louvre, Paris
6/14/2017

Holland (Netherlands)

The people really did wear wooden shoes!

Interestingly, this shoe thing was in many European villages. To this day, it is well-mannered to remove your shoes before entering a home. Many homes have slippers for you to put on when visiting. The farms and houses are often together, so this is a healthy tradition.

I always thought that Holland was a country. It is not. Holland is the name of a large region in the Netherlands. Many people from the Netherlands call themselves Dutch, and Dutch is the language of the country. Anyway, they love Americans, dogs, and the simple life! I love their chocolate, crepes, the people, and their flowers! I got treats all day long! *Bedankt*! (Thanks!)

When you go, you must go to one of the largest displays of flowers in Europe! Keukenhof has more than seven million blooms! It is amazing to see! The gardens stretch out over almost eighty acres! My mom's favorite flowers are peonies and tulips, but there are literally millions of different flowers. When you are in Keukenhof's gardens, you are just a few kilometers from Amsterdam, Netherlands. The whole town was built on stilts at one time!

French fry shops are everywhere! If you like Hunt's ketchup, bring your own, these folks eat their fries with mayonnaise or something like it.

Another cool thing to discover is the fort at Bourtange. It is shaped like an overlapping five-pointed star over another star. How did they do this between the 1500s to 1800s?

Hallo! *Welkom kom terug*! (Hello! Welcome and come back!)

Coming Home

We were so excited about coming back home to America! Although Delta Airlines was nice to me, our ride home was nothing like a commercial flight! We flew in with the guys and gals from the Ohio Air National Guard. We got to sleep in sleeping bags! It was amazing! After visiting my grandma and family in Kentucky, we made our way to Starkville, Mississippi! As we drove up, we saw small American flags lining our driveway and yellow ribbons on all the big trees in the front yard! I think the Smith side of the family has been remarkably busy. We loved it!

Our first trip away from home was to Biloxi, Mississippi. The Mississippi coast is home to Pops's only remaining aunt, Linda. We had a blast with her family and ate the traditional shrimp gumbo and rice.

Biloxi was actually ruled by England from 1763 to 1779! Then the Spanish came and conquered the area, ruling from 1779 to 1798! There is a beautiful lighthouse there, it is almost two hundred years old. There is a little island there that is called Dog Key Island! Another interesting fact about this small town is that it has been home to Barq's Root Beer since 1898!

It has been so crazy around here because of the COVID-19 restrictions and fears, so travel is very restrictive and no hugging! Everyone is scared. We can't be close to anyone; we miss our families and friends. The only place to go is camping because you can stay away from people and eat your own food. We went to Dauphin Island in July. I did not see any dauphins swimming in the ocean but, I saw some at a neat Estuarium. We were right across from the U.S. Coast Guard and got to watch their ships return and dock every day around sunset.

I still walk by my friend Ty's house. I stop and look down his driveway, but he is gone. He was an incredibly good friend. You know, you really need to love the humans around you and all animals. We can do just about anything we want to do, so let's always be kind. We all can listen more to each other and know that taking a nap is a good thing. Taking naps with someone who loves you is excellent! Naps are a great time to remember all the places you have been and dream of all the places you want to go to.

Okay, I nearly forgot to tell you the story about the goose, soldiers and, the town gate at Gangelt (from a chapter titled "Stinker Has to Fly").

The famous map maker or cartographer, Gerald Kremer, lived here during his childhood. The city is old, and it is first mentioned in the king's papers dated back in AD 828. Parts of the massive wall are still surrounding the town. Many times, this little town was beaten and ruled by different kings.

So when you come to the city from Geilenkirchen, you will see the walls on both sides of the road. The next sight is a big bronze goose with a carrot in its mouth standing in a fountain. This fountain stands in front of our favorite ice cream and bakeshop named after Kremer.

The locals' tell the story that the soldiers on guard had eaten and drank too much one night during a holiday. Their job was to watch the town's gate. Well, when they could no longer hold their heads up, they went to lock the gate. They realized they had lost the key and began to look for it without success. Having not eaten a carrot brought to them for supper, they decided to place the carrot in the gate's latch and take a short nap.

"Everything will be okay," they told each other.

A hungry goose came by and saw the delicious carrot; he ate the whole thing! "How nice," he said to himself as he waddled off to his nearby farm.

The soldiers were awakened by loud noises, and the sound of horses coming through the open gate! The enemies were upon them, and there was nothing they could do.

What is the moral of the story?

I think the moral of the story is, every good guardsman or guardswoman, must have a guard dog!

Update on Gangelt, Germany

Sadly, about four months after we left Germany, Gangelt was designated as Germany's hot zone for the coronavirus. Gangelt is the first to celebrate Oktober Fest, and the first to begin Carnival Week in January. This year, these celebrations brought deadly consequences. We are praying for America to find a cure. We are praying for wisdom, comfort, and peace.

A Note from My Mom

Adopting a pet is a big decision. Make sure you have a space in your heart and family for this precious animal. Some can be trained to be a medical assist dog while others can be trained to be service dogs. All can be house-trained. Here are some sad statistics I read from the aspca.org page:

1. Approximately 6.5 million companion animals (pets) enter U.S. animal shelters nationwide every year.
2. Approximately 1.5 million shelter animals are euthanized a year!

I encourage you to adopt your next pet versus buying one from a person or pet store. Selling pets is undoubtedly a lucrative business. Certain breeds lead both professional and amateurs to breed dogs for hundreds of dollars. It is a free country, so you have a choice.

Adoption is a selfless, brave, and a decision that will fill your heart. For me, pets are a reminder of God's unconditional love toward us.

Remagen, Germany

The Louvre, Paris, France

Paris' Eifel Tower, France

Netherlands

Paris, France

Geilenkirchen's Castle, Germany

M. N. Smith

Thorn, Netherlands

North Sea Beach, Belgium

Gillrath, Germany

M. N. Smith

Keukenhof Gardens, Holland

DeHaan, Belgium

Bruge, Belgium

Monschau, Germany

Bruge, Belgium

Monschau, Germany

Cologne, Germany

Zurich, Switzerland

Gangelt, Germany

Gerette!: The Adventures of a Mississippi Dog in Europe   43

About the Author

M. N. Smith was born in Louisville, Kentucky, and grew up in Honduras's remote jungles. She has earned a Bachelor of Science degree from the college of education and a master of science degree from the college of education at Mississippi State University. Smith has also earned a specialist in education from the University of Southern Mississippi.

CPSIA information can be obtained
at www.ICGtesting.com
Printed in the USA
BVHW021017090821
613997BV00019B/850

9 781637 105986